DIVINE PURPOSE

DIVINE PURPOSE

Discovering Your Calling in God's Plan

MARLOWE SINCLAIR

ArcanaVerse Books

CONTENTS

First Printing, 2024

CHAPTER 1

Introduction

Discovering the existence of a personal mission throughout so many existences increased the participants' thirst for knowledge, even centuries after they left the school of the Lemurian pathfinders. Thousands of lives, such as those of Abraham, Jacob, and Joseph, the basis for Israel - the promised supreme nation - became a need upon the called ones' very lives lifetimes. Discovering a life path, which would naturally make them grow as human beings and allow for the light they carried in their essence to illuminate the path of those around them, became a vital force, a blessed desire for sharing. These learned participants - men and women - focused their actions on increasing human awareness so that people could accept the consolatory truth and bypass life's formidable test. To pass and renew, they united themselves with the spiritual world on Earth, through the light of the eternal creator. Only then did they realize that their calling went beyond their definition of daily life. Their established purpose in this life existence would guide the way for others, enhancing the path towards his kingdom.

The creator has a plan for his creatures. Some people have very specific roles, like Noah, who was delegated to build an ark, on God's command, to save a remnant of special creatures. Others are to receive an idea which may germinate and grow into a powerful light. Such is the case of Noah's wife, who encouraged him to build the ark; her words, spoken out of pure love, germinated the seed of understanding planted in Noah's heart, allowing it to fully and completely spread its roots. Her unerring trust and unwavering faith not just cemented and sealed her intimate divine connection, but also helped supply infallible support in the face of potential disbelief of others. Such a release, motivated by pure love and the fervor in one's heart, planted itself like a genetically modified seed, allowing the light to witness its powerful, living connection in God's protection cage. Noah's wife was the one to inspire the planting of the seed and watched the miraculous chain of events unfold.

CHAPTER 2

Understanding Divine Purpose

Passion is an inner driving force that mobilizes a person to action when the intellect is in a state of paralysis. Being in the midst of a group of people wanting to demonstrate their authority over Him, Jesus bent down and inscribed with His finger in the ground: the image of the people that are without sin performing their legitimate task of punishment. This action revealed a single truth known to all: they realized their fault and left the woman alone. This is the action motivated by creativity, the paraphrasing of a divine fact without the noise of the rhythms of the Old Testament. We call it direct action on the part of God. The same signature as the one on divine creation many years before, when the human race had reached a dead end. The vacuum created by the intellect must be filled with divine purpose.

Understanding divine purpose. Most people assume that they walk in their divine calling because they like what they are doing. It is the lack of true passion that gets them thinking that maybe they have chosen the wrong career. However, competence should never be used as an indication of a person's calling. Even within the environment of a major decision, competence should be tested and only excellence should be tolerated. This means that one first learns his calling, then tests it within the major and minor decisions of his life. Can he excel at what he has prioritized in his life? God's plan is according to His divine purpose. The conviction that one has a political calling while being in the medical profession will lead to laziness, the failure in even passing.

CHAPTER 3

Reflecting on Your Life

Entering the silence of yourself defines your unique pattern of meaning (or purpose). Before the next section, find a time for going on the Inner Quest of silence and solitude. You may call this meditation, contemplation, quiet time, morning/evening pause, listening for God's voice, or getting in touch with your soul. This is the most important activity for humans. You are more than worth this time. You learn who you are and why God loves you. I encourage you to immerse yourself in the freedom of soulful silence 15 minutes a day and the 12 steps. What new insight has God given you about who you are and what you are meant to do?

As you look back over your life, do certain incidents or themes stand out? What has brought you joy or scared you? What have people commented on about you? These give clues about your unique pattern of meaning. The song of your heart has stirred over many years. Just as the symphony of a great composer is completed through countless rehearsals, our lives fine-tune their harmonies until the final movement. No matter where you are in life, now is the time to appreciate the glorious present of who you are as the world prepares to enjoy the melody of you for all eternity.

Seeking God's Guidance

It can be hard to pray for God's direction in your life — not because prayer is hard, but because praying to be shown your divine purpose can be terrifying. It's like opening Pandora's Box; what if there's not enough purpose to go around and God offers you some kind of otherworldly blue-light special on non-essential stuff no one else wants? Or worse, what if there already is a pink slip, and you've missed the purpose boat altogether because you were too busy thumbing through the summer beach reading specials at Walmart? If we ask God His plan for us, He might tell us, and what then? There may be much required of us, and in these orders, we might be asked to change, to be brave, to fight, to fail. Or He might not tell us anything.

If you've been raised in the church, then you have likely heard some version of the following advice for finding your calling a hundred times or more: "Seek God's direction for your life." But what, exactly, does that mean? When I was in high school, I remember talking to a friend who was starting to feel a pull toward the college campus ministry where I worked. "What do I do?" she asked. I told her, "Pray and ask God where he wants you." At the time, her question felt momentous to me. Now I fear my answer might have seemed like one of those Church answers we youth-group kids liked to mock: "Thank you, Captain Obvious."

CHAPTER 5

Embracing Your Gifts and Talents

Energy in the form of faith, the foundation of divine nature, never weakens. Divine encouragement inspires and fills hearts, starting to believe in unpleasant circumstances. With the power of transformation, everyone becomes closer to the divine ideal and the circle of knowledge. Through knowledge, we will be transfigured: we will get the fire of change. Keeping its glow, divine attention kindles and constructs personalities and the universe. We find and get the fire of change, and knowledge flows to eternal life.

Divine encouragement gives us an opportunity to open our hearts and accept enthusiasm and confidence in beliefs that inspire love, faith, and hope; hunger for truth and thirst for God.

Trust means belief, conviction, security, and a feeling that promises warrant reliability and responsibility. When we rely on God, we allow ourselves to make God-ordained decisions. This inspires us to do what God desires with all our heart, mind, and soul for His pleasure. Like quadrants of a circle, each decision falls into God-embedded destiny.

Embracing your gifts and talents, by revealing the truth about our true essence, God teaches us how to walk in divine nature and breathe in our destiny. He shows the way and affirms His promise, saying:

"Everyone shall be happy and fulfilled, and trust me, everything will be revealed to you."

CHAPTER 6

Overcoming Challenges

David was thirty years old when he began to reign, and he reigned forty years. At Hebron, he reigned over Judah seven years and six months, and at Jerusalem, he reigned over all Israel and Judah thirty-three years. Your divine purpose, if you trace it back far enough (and I pray you can go even further than this), proceeds from the God who preexisted before time ever began and was quietly conceived even before that. He is your divine architect, silent partner, benevolent investor, and skillful maestro of your entire "op" business. Without him, the "op" concept would have remained mute. Quiet, unnamed, unnoticed, and never even brought to birth, it would have terminated before it even began, still in its conception.

When it comes to purpose, challenges are inevitable. But David's great passion for the God who gave him both calling and currency is what fueled his tenacious persistence, absolute trust, and abiding confidence as he faced down his life-threatening challenges. When David enters your everyday life, you will be better prepared to overcome your obstacles as you cling to his God. In these three verses from 2 Samuel 5:4-5, for example, we discover what David endured to march into divine purpose: years of unknowns, his life leveraged into a pon, and an undivided leader's calling ultimately contested by a violent enemy.

CHAPTER 7

Taking Action Towards Your Purpose

God granted a great future to David through sanctifying the present, but he uses the same "ruthless scrutiny" as with us. Through the hardness of battles with adversaries, we claim the prize with bittersweet exclamation. Our true calling, our vocation, is what the divine poetry engraves on our hearts by warfare, not what current challenges and peripheral conflicts scream. The difficult part is to recognize this persistent urging burden in our lives. George Bernard Shaw once wrote, "This is the true joy in life, the being used for a purpose recognized by yourself as a mighty one; the being a force of Nature instead of a feverish, selfish little cloud of ailments and grievances complaining that the world will not devote itself to making you happy. I am of the opinion that my life belongs to the whole community, and as long as I live, it is my privilege to do for it whatever I can. I want to be thoroughly used up when I die, for the harder I work, the more I live."

If we are truly open to the guidance of the Spirit in our lives, we can be led to our purpose. In reading the Scriptures, praying, thinking of others first, and being patient, we can create the right mental attitude of expectancy, openness, and responsiveness. As children of God, living out a personal vocational call always develops community around us. We are not brought to a purpose alone. Instead, we come to our purpose in relationships. This God of relationship, the Trinity, plants the seed of our calling in a person and nurtures it to fruition in networked relationships. Just as it took "a village to raise a child," it takes a community to form a leader. In fact, the relationship to a certain network is often the way we recognize our individual pleading.

CHAPTER 8

Finding Fulfillment in God's Plan

Divine Purpose focuses on discovering and applying one's God-given biblical purpose in society, largely through worker roles. The book begins by examining the texts of redemption in Revelation and by pointing out that, if non-believers aren't distinguished by their intelligence, mannerisms, work type, involvement in ministry, or how they spend money, then non-believers who lack a sense of mission can be distinguished from the believers who work and serve their communities. Even for Christians who recognize that they have a calling, planning to learn about one's calling in a post-layoff season can seem like a less spiritual matter. For many Christians, a Gallup survey from 2019 has revealed that the struggle to discuss an unequivocal vocation has become one of the least spiritual, non-usage-of-time difficulties. The birthing of Divine Purpose: Discovering Your Unique Calling as a consequence of conversations and prior reflections on career discernment principally exists in the secular-rejection sphere. The book reads as a response to these struggles.

Divine Purpose: Discovering Your Calling in God's Plan primarily aims to help believers filter their sense of professional calling through an understanding of church work and believers' roles in society and addresses the disconnect many Christians feel between their secular work life and church work. This guidebook is especially appropriate for evangelical readers who might grapple with perceiving their work and secular life as less meaningful than those of individuals who pursue a divine, unique, ecclesiastical vocation. Martinez teaches seminary at a prominent evangelical institution and has also written for a Latinx audience in Spanish and English language outlets and in his book The Gospel-Shaped Work: Serving God Both in Secular and Varied Ecclesiastical Vocations. Martinez completed a Ph.D. in Practical Theology at Southeastern Baptist Theological Seminary and a ThM in Pastoral Leadership and Biblical Exposition at Western Seminary, and he teaches demographic patterns of pastors in California and health and religious factors influencing pastor retention and job satisfaction.

Building a Supportive Community

I was teaching school at the time and had learned through preparation for that career, a tremendously beneficial thought-changing behavior. Instead of griping about how my friend was acting, I said to Raymond, "You have been a good friend to Joanna and me. I am concerned about her well-being and I have to go back to school to study in both my bachelor degree area and my teaching profession. If I am to be a loving friend to Joanna that she deserves to have, I need to develop compassion and patience." Towards the end of the year, I was so exhausted from school and emotional from building a support system that the conversation I ended up having with Raymond defeated me. Charles was as calm as a lake, and with a very large sigh, he quietly said to me, "I think that the right thing to do in this situation would be to tell your friend that too much has been going on in your life recently, and that if some things have had to take some of her attention away from your friendship. Therefore, you have been diligently working so hard to prepare for a promising and successful future at becoming a teacher! You have been and still are giving Conscious Leadership 1,000% of your best effort to improve a better you in helping those in all walks of life."

If you're not already connected, where do you go to find other people? Churches, colleges, workplaces, volunteer organizations, athletic teams

– the possibilities are almost endless. Distance and age no longer have to be barriers; the Internet brings people from all over the globe right into our homes. Searching the net can be used to find people from your neighborhood, people who share your ideas and interests, and people interested in the same causes you're passionate about. You have to look for them and be open to accepting invitations. Be realistic about making and maintaining relationships. Know how many good friends you can have. After moving to my home shortly after my first husband died, I was confronted by a woman whom I had never met. We became good friends fairly quickly and started socializing with her partner. We really enjoyed our friendship together for a long time. Then I began to notice it was consisting of her wanting to do things together and requiring someone to listen to her very personal life too much of the time. It became more like work for me than a pleasure. Also, there was a personality trait I enjoyed when we were friends that began to turn into something that irritated her husband.

Life moves in the direction of the friends you hang out with, for better or for worse. This is a statistical fact. Knowing you weren't designed to live your life alone, building a circle of support around you is absolutely one of the most important tasks you'll ever undertake. Lacking in this respect undermines our chance of satisfaction in every other area of our lives. Connecting with the right people empowers you to reach your highest potential. Lonely people are living in a totally different world than the connected person. The world isn't a different place. But it feels different. It can feel more oppressive, more danger-ous, more demanding. Conversely, a support system can make demands easier, make the world an easier place to navigate, and make us feel more comfortable within it. Lonely people literally and figuratively do not have someone "on their side." They feel responsibility more keenly with no one to help shoulder the burden.

CHAPTER 10

Nurturing Your Spiritual Growth

Another important aspect of growing spiritually is to use your gifts and talents within your church and your community. There is always a need for volunteers to help prepare a church dinner or work at a shelter or crisis center. It will also help you to see others living out their faith, which in turn will help you to see the importance of living your faith daily. Another good way to grow closer to God is to read and listen to religious authors. There are many generations of holy men and women who have written about their faith life that we may also grow in our own faith. Just think, if everyone followed at least one of these five suggestions, what a colossal difference it would make in everyone's spiritual walk with the Lord. In no time, that conversation will become gratitude for all the blessings you receive on a daily basis from a loving Heavenly Father.

You must never be satisfied with your spiritual growth until the day the Lord calls you home. We must strive with everything within us to strengthen our relationship with our Heavenly Father. What can you do to grow spiritually? The first step is to develop a regular habit of Bible reading, prayer, and church attendance. As suggested in prayer is like talking to a friend, and for the first time it may take a conscious act to have this conversation, but as you continue to talk, the conversation seems to flow easier. In order to develop a close friendship with a person, we have to spend considerable time with that person. The same is true with the Heavenly Father. We must make time to talk with Him every day. You need to develop the same habit of Bible reading and church attendance.

CHAPTER 11

Balancing Your Divine Purpose with Other Responsibilities

The Savior, with a divine center, maintained a perfect balance of love, insight, discernment, foresight, and trust in God, with both spirit and mind, supplying detonating and pulsating movement, and grace to everything he did. Another example of perfect balance was Mary, Martha's sister, mentioned in Luke 10:42. "Mary hath chosen that good part," the Lord Jesus said, "which shall not be taken away from you." Mary had chosen to sit at the feet of Jesus and hear his word. Jesus did not reprimand Martha for her genuine hospitality and efforts in serving when he said, "Martha, Martha, thou art careful and troubled about many things: but one thing is needful: and Mary hath chosen that good part, which shall not be taken away from her." Mary and Martha inhabited different roles and responsibilities in serving the Lord, but fully exercised them both so that they are remembered as examples of love and service in the church of Christ to come.

No5: To teach about balance in your life, I think the best place to start is to ask the question, "What did the perfect balance of Jesus Christ look like, and how can I achieve this?" In his ministry on earth, the Lord Jesus Christ was the most perfectly balanced of all people. He "went about doing good" (Acts 10:38), successfully carrying out his divine work, while being a loving and exemplary family member. Despite frequent distractions, the Savior knew he had received his divine purpose from God (Acts 17:7-8). "The Son can do nothing of Himself, but what He sees the Father do; for whatever He does, the Son also does in like manner" (John 5:19). He taught, "My meat is to do the will of him that sent me, and to finish his work" (John 4:34).

The importance of balance. After you accept your divine purpose—your God-ordained calling—you will want to ask, "How do I fulfill my divine purpose and at the same time be the best person I can be: a good wife or husband, parent, child, grandparent, friend, church and community volunteer, and worker or employer?" To be aware of your high calling is a tremendous advantage. But you may now be overwhelmed with all there is to be and do to fulfill your purpose. In some cases, with good intentions, you may experience frustration, anxiety, and unrealistic stress in seeking to fulfill your calling. Here you will learn to balance your responsibilities with your divine purpose. You will learn not only how to fill your roles and responsibilities as a good servant of Christ and member of the body, but also about "the best part" gracing your life with poise and peace. Then you can prayerfully serve the Lord and others, in love, with all your heart. And your high calling will have its intended beauty and result.

CHAPTER 12

Trusting in God's Timing

Despite this problem, those who follow Jesus know more about God than most nonbelievers. Similarly, Christians are certainly closer to God than they were before they accepted salvation through Jesus Christ. Since believers know that God is just, loving, and orchestrating events to prepare for His glory, they are better prepared to put their trust in His decisions. Psalm 27:13, 14 says, "What if I had not believed that I would see the goodness of the Lord in the land of the living! Wait on the LORD; be of good courage, and He shall strengthen your heart; wait, I say, on the LORD!" The writer seeks God's assistance and knows that his trust in the Lord's judgment will help him overcome this obstacle. There are a number of things we can do to help develop our trust in God's sense of timing so that we will demonstrate that trust towards others and develop our relationship with God even more.

The Bible often describes God as longsuffering with us and asks us to be patient with others. This is usually not a problem unless our patience concerns a matter near to our hearts, such as an answered prayer or something else we may be looking forward to. In ancient Palestine, there was a popular saying reflecting this sentiment: "I pray that the Lord is patient." This may show that believers have never been very patient when it comes to that which they desire. This is similar to saying, "I'm praying for patience, and I want it now." We say we are waiting on God or His timing, but our actions show almost no trust that God knows what He is doing or that He has things under control.

CHAPTER 13

Staying Focused and Disciplined

Taking the Lord on as your partner acknowledges that you are not alone in this. In partnership with God, we acknowledge that it is no longer about the toil but the triumph; it is not about what we have to give, it's about what we have the privilege of receiving. We must realize that our abilities are not our own. When God calls people, He gifts them in a way that equips them for their purpose in life. The closer and more aware we are about divine purpose, the more aware we are that whatever effort is made to fulfill it isn't because we thought of doing it on our own. We realize that there is something else working within us to keep us going. Using gifts that have been given, we partner with God to create a reality of maximum impact and effectiveness – such sweet victory speaks to divine purpose.

I know you sometimes feel that living God's perfect purpose for your life is a grueling drudgery and that the burden of living in His will is a thankless toil. There are times in my own life when I feel that it is too hard to live in the center of God's will. The task seems too monumental. I would start to believe that it is impossible and decide to take a break. I would dole out self-help to myself and get distracted with what the world is saying. But days later when life gets tough and I become weary, the calling would start to tug at me again. At those times, a gentle voice would remind me that thankless drudgery full of weariness never comes from God. What I was subscribing to wasn't His plan. I didn't have the kind of faith that I needed to keep me driven.

CHAPTER 14

Cultivating a Positive Mindset

One of the verses the Holy Spirit recently used to nudge me back to a positive frame of mind graces our lake house dining room walls. I had seen it for the umpteenth time when, boom, He spoke to me. The title for this photo comes from an Enya song – The Longships – that I am told is about Vikings who brought chaos wherever they went. The Holy Spirit explained that God's instructions to Joshua provide sound advice on how to prosper when things look their darkest – let Him guide us securely, dedicate whatever we do to His service, and then hold on and watch Him establish us. The only way that the troubles of life enslave us is if we give them our power and then obey their demands by living only as the dust of the earth. God did not give anyone that authority. Instead, He gave each of us Ruth 1:9 and Ezekiel 22:30-31 authority.

Chapter 14 covers mindset, gratitude, the link between our thoughts, emotions, feelings, and actions, and the role the Holy Spirit plays in empowering us to develop a positive mindset. This chapter mentions the first step in the Cultivating a Positive Mindset strategy that the Holy Spirit shared with us: practice gratitude. It lets the Holy Spirit talk more about the link between our thoughts, emotions, feelings, and actions. The case we make is that as I am, so will the world seem to be. The third step in the strategy is to repeat God's assurances out loud. Even when we know that Luke 1:37 does not say, "Brussels sprouts will be established," it is charged with power. Our current circumstances can weigh us down.

CHAPTER 15

Embracing Change and Adaptability

While our core message remains the same, the way it is communicated should change and adapt. It could be the presentation, an example, the topic's perspective, use of new technology, or even the stylistic approach you take. You have acquired much wisdom from your surroundings and with this wisdom, your understanding of the world as a whole has grown, so why not your individual perspective or voice? You may find yourself taking the information your mentors have provided you, filtering it through God's Word, your prayerful meditation, and what you have learned on your spiritual quest of the Word. This will allow you to take the holistic world view and teaching back to others in a new and unique way. The teaching through new mediums and related methods such as virtual meeting rooms, Word Art, and the resurgence of expressive poetic narrative or painting might be different. You would take your unique wisdom and shape it within the current context of experience and thought. In finding genuine human feelings and stories so all-encompassing, you are at once deeper into the Word and deeper into the person to be served. You might be surprised that by reaching deeper into the Good News, in your unique and original message, you can reach greater heights in your diverse world audience.

So how do we reconcile the knowledge and pursuit of our individual calling while our ultimate focus remains on the spread of the Good News? The way we live our daily lives. We truly live out the second great commandment by discovering and living out our individual assignments. We aren't thinking about what we will get, but about serving God and then others. We serve God by finding and living out the specific purpose He has for us as we intersect with His universal plan.

CHAPTER 16

Overcoming Fear and Doubt

When faced with truth versus lies, sin versus false beliefs, our growth will wane without God. Doubts based upon our circumstances will evaporate our wings. A life not grafted will inevitably bear bad fruit, as it can only rest upon its parent instead of drinking from the Son. The vine will sustain neither the shallow roots nor the dense foliage. They will struggle to bear the weight as He alone gives purpose, making us into the trellises of His master garden.

When we do not nurture a walk with God or fail to create a strong spiritual foundation from the outset, we develop a shaky faith easily rattled by the world, people, and even our emotions. When we attempt to steady our spiritual life with our fruitless efforts, we weave a rootless life into our fragile spiritual tapestry. Adversity kills horizontal religious acts. If our limbs can't grasp ahold of God or shore up against Him because of our shallow roots, they die. With the loss of opportunity, our roots grow deeper. Pain reveals our shallow roots. When God stands at the edge of disability, asking us to trust Him above the confusion and helplessness, we reproach our doubts. That act of faith helps us grow stronger. Only God can thicken our spiritual roots to sustain real growth.

We are to live a life worthy of God's calling. We are to lead a life at work and home that sets a standard for others to follow. This is how we shine our light in response to God's grace. This is what glorifies God.

CHAPTER 17

Aligning Your Actions with Your Purpose

Do more mainline Christian activities that will give you a better sense of what being, doing, and having are really right for you. You can't just sit back and wait for your dream job; you must work to figure out what God calls you to do, what special benefit you provide for the body your own "piece of sand." Just as missionaries are unable to bring Jesus to unreached people unless the people become well enough to overcome their resistance, so also we cannot share Jesus to the hungry people in our "piece of sand" unless we show them a better way to live that needs faith in Christ. But don't overdo it. Don't get involved with an outreach where you have so much to do that you would cause further harm to yourself or your family. Only accept a place where the powerful spirit of God is already at work.

Make sure you've got a good grip on the five basics of your life: God, your commitments of callings for living for Jesus, your spouse, your family, and your friends in descending order of priority. Your priorities for pleasing Jesus should be first, then making your marriage a great love affair with your spouse, followed by raising your kids in the nurture of the Lord, and finally contributing to the well-being of friends and other people.

CHAPTER 18

Serving Others with Love and Compassion

Mercy to the suffering, help to those who are unfortunate, and sympathy for the distressed is sent alike to the worthy and the unworthy, and this is the greatest revelation of the character of divinity. The Lord always rules and reigns as being high and lifted up, and makes ready to receive from men the offers of their hearts. Man can give to the God of heaven but little, save human affection and human love, but as these do not lessen the value of the gifts of gold and silver, so they cannot lessen the value and power of the intercession on behalf of men. Only those who minister with a loving spirit and feeling can, or will, be companions with the Lord at His table, and with fervor offer up the petitions and desires of their hearts. Only with faith can the children of men strive to lay up worldly treasures for the last great day. The sympathy between the human and the divine will awaken in the believers of truth an assurance that by their acts of kindness to one another their influence has not been wholly lost upon sinners.

The Samaritan's compassion was expressed and made known to the wounded and dying man by the intense interest and fervent zeal that he cherished for his salvation. The good Samaritan's selfless and practical legislation furnishes an enduring object lesson for the whole human race. It encourages the exercise of mercy and brotherly love from all of Christ's disciples today. Christ Himself ministered to humanity, and while on earth He was constantly ministering to the distressed of every class. The Lord Jesus Christ practiced the loving-kindness He wishes His followers to practice. It is a solemn truth that the personification of all mercy, compassion, and benevolence is Jesus Christ, and that no love can or could ever compare with His.

CHAPTER 19

Celebrating Your Unique Journey

Let what you value drive you, but understand that conflict is the evidence that you have integrated your best work and life. The only way to escape conflict is to stop creating and giving value to your world. Without value, you cannot serve those around you. Value always places before us questions and challenges that force us to grow. What questions are pressing on your heart? Which areas of your life are challenged to be true to themselves? Can you see your conflict as proof of a life lived fully? Let's allow our unique self to take center stage: your personality, your abilities, and your reignited gifts for ministry and your community. You are a masterpiece!

We spent the better part of this book uncovering the myths that deceive us, the barriers that stand in our way of fulfilling our purpose, and the truths that will help us unleash our best life. Our journey toward purpose begins as we discover how deeply loved we are, right here and right now. This knowledge gives a deep spiritual assurance to our soul that cannot be limited by the noise and smoke of life surrounding us. Purpose driven by love will never be corrupted, corroded, or consumed. Remember, God's purposes for your life are yours to have and to hold.

CHAPTER 20

Surrendering to God's Will

Jesus Christ truly is the savior. He saved us - and continues to save us - because every day he passes through history and through our lives. His name is the Savior; and he saves us with his help, with his power. He saves us because, every day, he passes through us, caring for us. The care of Jesus for us never ends. And for him to take us on his path and save us, what do we need? Surrendering to his love, allowing him to take us to the next level, allowing him to save us. Christ wishes to move us to new realms. Surrendering to Christ is a journey of loving trust, utilizing Christ's heart to purify our personal heart. Through confiding dialogue, sharing thoughts and feelings with him, surrendering means uniting our own will with the Lord's, incorporating his desires into our own, transforming self-rule into a relationship based on mutual trust.

Christ energizes the universe. Jesus keeps it alive and holds it together. Our planet and all of nature constantly experience the power flow of the Creator. Though sometimes we feel as if life is flowing without direction, we benefit from the divine propulsion. He guides us through life, though generally incognito. Precisely because of his anonymity, our steps are important. They allow God to lead history to its end. Even when we berate God for never letting man decide anything, his silence expresses his profound respect for our freedom. God never reveals himself to us without our initiative. He waits for us to seek him;

he wants us to come to him, to ask him for his advice. He wants to help us accomplish our purpose and our mission. For that, he waits. Once he manifests himself, he asks that we let him take the reins of history so mankind can reach its goal.

Finding Peace and Contentment

A Message From Chapter 21 - Finding Peace and Contentment: Our search for peace and contentment need not be a doomed, lifelong quest! Instead, we have the capacity to put that search permanently to rest, by discovering and embracing her true identity and purpose. The fact that we can reach a deep and abiding sense of peace should not be in doubt. God also wants us to be happy, contented, and at peace, and is most willing to give us the essential peace that we need. God is here to help us, in every aspect of our lives, and indeed strongly desires to do so. Why would this be true? It is because we are an unimaginable joy to God! We are to be integral components in His forevermore plan. Our peace and well-being are key objectives of everything that God does. Our personal peace and well-being are a tangible expression of God's undeniable compassion and infinite love!

To illustrate the tremendous security provided through our association with God and His divine plan, we quote excerpts from God's description of His chosen city, Jerusalem, by the prophet Zephaniah. He wrote: "The Lord is in the city, and where is no peer, and He shall show in that day that I am to allay that afflict thee, and gather her that was cast out, and I will get them praise and honor in every land, where they have been put to confusion. At the time, when I will bring you again: and at the time, when I will gather you together: for I will give you a name, and praise among all the people of the earth, when I shall have brought back your captivity before your eyes," saith the Lord. God is within her, she shall not be moved: God will help her at the dawn of morning.

How does one find peace and contentment in life? This is certainly not an easy challenge for us to undertake. However, the solution is often tied to the divine guidance given to us by our ever-loving and ever-present God. He provides a secure path for our journey to finding the peace we seek.

CHAPTER 22

Honoring Your Divine Purpose in Relationships

Divine purpose and destiny are often presented in the church as personal matters between a believer and God. While we receive individual direction from God, our divine purpose plays an integral role in the conquest of God's global purpose, and the two cannot be dissociated. If we are going to fulfill our divine purpose, we must also complete the role we were born to play in God's great play. In this role, we may be assigned to provide powerful prayer support for the front-line ministers of God's world, or we may be needed to finance God's great moves, or we may need to be sent as missionaries to treat the sick, despairing, and spiritually dead on the battlefield; whatever role we play, our joint performance can bring about the fulfillment of God's destiny for the nations. For those of us who have been apprehending and employing the revelation of our own divine purpose and spiritual gifts, it may come as no surprise when my assertion that your divine purpose is not just about you but also about God's great purpose should kick in. After all, our divine skills are supposed to be exercised to the benefit of the Body of Christ (1 Pet. 4:10), and God's global purpose may involve benefiting the church. Yet many need reminders or confirmation of this truth, and the aim of this chapter is to further establish people's belief in something that has been declared for centuries.

In this dynamic book "Blending Faith with Finances," the Matthews takes you on an insightful, practical, and revelatory journey regarding money from a biblical perspective. As Christians, the younger generation and those to come must begin to shift their mindset, not only about money but about life in general. In this renowned book, the Matthews draw a line in the sand on some of the long-standing religious and denominational myths about money. This book gives the readers a blueprint on seeking out the real truth about their finances and provides them with plenty of practical application. As Christians, we must deal with money both in how it relates to the church and also how it should be dealt with in our own personal lives. The Matthews allow the reader to release themselves from the bondage of believing that money doesn't affect their spiritual walk with Christ. The Bible says in Romans 8:1 that there is "no condemnation to them who are in Christ Jesus." As a believer, you are obligated to be a good steward over your money, and this book will give you examples of how to do just that.

CHAPTER 23

Cultivating Gratitude and Appreciation

In churches across this country, worship dedicated to the practice of appreciation has been held. This practice, led by the Reverend Tim Morales, is held on the third Sunday of each month and focuses on living daily in a grateful heart, and the results are spectacular. But there are also other ways of learning to appreciate our lives. Scientists have discovered that when we practice appreciation, we activate parts of the brain associated with reward, joy, and pleasure. It reduces cortisol and stress and adds resilience. It also helps us acquire more social interactions and promotes prosocial behavior. For example, consider the following guidelines, which are based on Dr. Tomas Lyubomirsky's research: Welcome each day with a grateful heart by starting a gratitude journal or expressing your gratitude, aloud, to your partner or some other person. Thank you, people, for your blessings. After recording your gratitude entries, think about how you have come to be grateful. This process increases appreciation and anticipation for the most important source of gratitude. Minimize daily problems and avoid becoming overwhelmed with tasks.

I once received a call from a church asking to borrow a bilingual minister for a funeral. They had checked with me months before, before I had found a job in our local hospital, and were under the impression that I was a "full-time" minister. When I explained my current situation, they hung up the phone and did not even send me a "thank you for your time." I understand that it can be disappointing when you are looking for services and people cannot meet your needs. But we should not allow details to cast a shadow over the great gift of life. As we immerse ourselves in our spiritual practice, as a community let's stop taking our problems and opportunities for granted and start being grateful for them because although at times our prayers may remain unanswered, we can continue to say and give thanks in the struggle, for he loves us, and when we turn, as this community, in appreciation and humility, we discover the comfort and direction that we need to touch and be touched by the love that flows through it.

CHAPTER 24

Embracing Personal Growth and Development

Self-improvement is the improvement of one's knowledge, status, or character by one's own efforts. This is not something that can be done by the pastor, the prophet, or the teacher alone, but also by each individual. Education never stops. The value of reading good books cannot be overemphasized. The benefits have been apparent in my own life as many times I have received the answer/book I needed in prayer for a situation I am going through. Reading, particularly one's personal Bible, allows your spirit to fill up and helps you to overflow into the world. Information empowers. Knowledge is the key to success in any area of life. Additionally, reading gives you a broader perspective. It also helps you to use your God-given gifts and talents to help others. Providing evidence on the reading-income relationship, Sayeed and Hossain (2020) outline that reading elevates poverty and strengthens the country's economy and increases human development.

One of my biggest fears is to have lived a lazy and unproductive life. When potential is not used, it is wasted. This simple adage is the reason I am always seeking to grow and develop myself. Ever thirsting for knowledge and understanding, I am constantly seeking a deeper and more passionate relationship with the Father. I continually set and achieve new goals for self-improvement by applying new lessons. We must strive to develop all the gifts that God has given us because growth and development are crucial to achieving our divine purpose.

CHAPTER 25

Discovering Your Passion and Mission

This book is dedicated to you, the person who is in a whirlwind of a struggle. Furthermore, to the person who constantly asks: Are my career goals aligned with the divine purpose for my life? What on earth am I passionate about? What can I do to prepare myself for the workplace of the future? The Lord desires for each one of us to have a sense of satisfaction in our occupation, accompanied by an eternal sense of significance to the spiritual significance in our lives. The word occupation comes from occupational affinity that describes jobs in which we can actively engage in activities we are most passionate about. It reminds us to do whatever glorifies God. Efficiently rendering an occupational purpose requires pursuing a career that is closely aligned to meeting the needs of His people while allowing them to experience the passion and calling in that work. In this chapter, I am going to provide you with some activities to assess whether or not you are going to have the right career. More importantly, I want you to measure yourself against these activities to affirm what you should do to prepare yourself for that career.

Let's say you already have an inkling of what makes your heart sing, what makes you sad, or what makes you angry. Discerning what you are passionate about is the second step to discovering your divine calling. It is the passion that God has woven into the very core of your being. It also reflects the interests that God has prompted in you. By identifying what is closest to your thoughts and what you have always wanted to achieve, you will embrace the direct path to your ultimate fulfillment. Your calling might have already been shaping up inside you without you realizing it. It is important to take time off by yourself to examine what you are passionate about, what gives meaning to your life, and what really keeps you going. Once you figure these things out, stick with them no matter what, and explore different ways. Divine surprises might also lie ahead.

CHAPTER 26

Seeking Wisdom and Guidance from Scripture

One of the nine rare personalities in the Bible was Job, the wealthy man who lost everything and went on to be known as the very name of patience and forbearance - not because patience and the gift of foreseeing were woven into his nature from birth, but because he developed them in his young age by the help of God. When disasters took away all his property and killed all his sons and daughters and left him alone, wounded and miserable, he unexpectedly bowed down to the earth and served in general, going to the state of mourning. When his wife and friends tried to put him in the wrong, he only spoke a few words: "The Lord hath sacrificed, the Lord hath given unto the Lord, the Lord hath taken away, just as it was pleasing." "...in this," says the Scripture, "Job did not sin by the impious." And this is quite likely if an intelligent and good educator stretches out his hand and says: "What are you saying? Shall we accept from the Lord only the blessings, and not accept adversities? Job, a righteous man, accepted the Lord's word; and from this sad event, until the end of his life, he did not murmur or speak any thoughtless or disdainful about God."

CHAPTER 27

Trusting in God's Provision

After hearing complaints from his people that they were thirsty, Moses pleaded to God with an anxious heart. Nervous and compressed, confusion and anger often occupy our thoughts. So, in these times of uncertainty, we can find our wanderings also filled with murmuring. Issuing a decree, God commanded Moses to strike a rock with his staff, which would cause the water to flow like a river. We are prompted to trust in the Lord while wandering and submit to His provision. Unless a seed falls into the ground and dies, it remains just parts of a plant; otherwise, without the planting, there would be no sizable harvest. Neither does water alone provide spiritual or physical restoration. How is dialogue and prayer with God alone sufficient for you? When there is silence in heaven, can we continue to be faithful and recognize Him? "And my God will supply every need of yours according to his riches in glory in Christ Jesus."

My precious believer, you feel secure in your place of employment or income; your sick loved one appears to be in stable health; your church serves your spiritual needs; or you may be experiencing peace during your season of caregiving. Imagine tomorrow. Would you feel disappointed, frustrated, or mourn for the life that was? Can you still trust God as He tests the foundation of your faith or trust that there is a spiritual perspective for the hardships you must endure? In Pharaoh's earliest dreams, he heard God's message. Instead of asking for deliverance, he cried out for aid from his magicians and wise men. You boldly declare who can interpret and see into my past on my behalf. God was patient, yet watched as the pharaoh's heart hardened. With repeated warnings and an overture of arguments, Pharaoh had many chances to obey, yet he believed he could get through this trial without God. He chooses not to trust in the God of Heaven.

"Trust in me with all your heart, and do not lean on your own understanding. In all your ways acknowledge me, and I will make your paths straight." Proverbs 3:5-6 NASB

CHAPTER 28

Overcoming Obstacles and Setbacks

Experiencing difficulty and adversity is natural. High achievers also know this. They are, however, not deterred by any obstacles. They meet challenges head-on and move forward. They emerge on the other side as stronger and better people. The person who knows how to overcome them can use any setback as road signs pointing toward the glorious life that is filled with those glorious truths. During adversity, people's real character is revealed. Choosing to be a better person means being able to embrace every difficulty that comes along. Difficulties are learning experiences that mold our character. When unexpected setbacks arise, stay focused on your goals. Become stronger people in the process. The choices you make can keep you focused or distract you from what is most important. Your choices reveal your priorities. Know that adversity makes you strong and keeps your character refined, assures that the path undertaken in pursuit of a goal is the right one. Do not quit at times of adversity. As a key step in achieving success, setbacks clarify and develop your character, thus preparing you to more effectively tackle future opportunities and challenges. Rely on them.

When God calls you to do something significant in His plan for humanity, as well as in your own life, you will face obstacles and setbacks. The bigger the call, the greater and more numerous the challenges. This is natural when God invites you to move beyond the ordinary. Satan, the great deceiver, senses that when God calls you, you are willing and will be an excellent target. But Satan does not have the last word, nor the most powerful hand. This book is based on many real opportunities missed or wasted due to their authors' and actors' own decisions or actions, or Satan's attacks. I hope that reading about them and the approach they did (or their disclosure) may inspire you not to do the same.

CHAPTER 29

Recognizing and Utilizing Opportunities

We must seek direction in life. We must take the opportunities that God presents us. Without seeking or following, God's special direction for us is certain to be missed. We encourage you to engage in the process of seeking His direction. The letter to the Philippians includes two wonderful verses that are frequently quoted as encouragement to us when we find ourselves in circumstances of uncertainty. Paul writes, "I can do all things through Christ who strengthens me (Philippians 4:13)". We often quote "I can do all things through Christ..." in our moments of challenge and frustration, but let's consider the surrounding context of the verse.

Before we begin, let's take a few minutes to review our concepts from past weeks. We need to remind ourselves that we are individually created with a special purpose. While we are similar in loving God, the ways in which we can show that love are as different as we are. We all desire God's plan to be revealed, but we have experienced times of discouragement, of lack of clarity of His plan for our future. There is no doubt that God has a good purpose for us. We can have confidence in that. But how could we know what the special purpose in God's plan is for us? "What shall I do?"

Will I ever have the big impact that I dream of? Will my life continue to be small and unimportant? How can I be sure I am doing God's will in the everyday normalcy that is called my life? Christine Hoover is answering these questions with The Grumbles. Julie Adlesberger is struggling with moving in a new direction. Lori says "I have that sensation that I am on the verge of a call, but I just can't see it yet!" We will devote this week's discussion to exploring practical ideas of how to navigate through the peaks and valleys of finding and following our directions.

Living a Life of Purpose and Meaning

Caution should be exercised in our understandings of human development, in understandings of attachment, relationship, the motivation to create families, etc. when they are defined primarily in biological and psychological forces. They are, according to this understanding and dogma, reflexivity and regression; the problem of the human being coming before itself. We must also be wary of the force of the "liberated" human will or of the therapeutic power of human imagination with no grounding or of a return to heteronomy. All life, the Jesuit Anthony de Mello liked to say, is "orthognosis", a "right grasp", of the situation where we find ourselves. The "problem", he continued, laughing, is "You don't know the problem". That ignorance is the dynamic and the root of all sin.

The way God made us to flourish is not an abstraction. Nothing in the mind of God is delusional or surreal. God only makes real, practical, functional, observable concepts, things, and beings at any level of God's creative activity. But now this primary attribute of everything God makes makes perfect sense. We are made as human beings to be most fully ourselves and to be happy when we are living our life according to the purpose for which we are made, and that purpose will be one that is for our greatest good, our greatest happiness. The way God made us to flourish is hardwired into us because it expresses the truth of who we are; what is real and true in our human nature. Suffering comes in the irreducibility between who we really are and how we are living. This call or divine purpose is the fundamental purpose and fundamental identity we have as rational beings, our "primary vocation", as John Paul II called it. If we do not intentionally work to live our life in accordance with that purpose, we will become the victims of our own genius; that genius God planted within us at the very moment we were created that is our very heart. The curse is the overwhelming sense of futility in life that results when we do not do what we were designed to be, the agonizing question, "what is my purpose?", is the most fundamental reality of human existence.

CHAPTER 31

Leaving a Legacy of Faith and Impact

What sort of legacy is God calling you to leave? Your legacy of faith can start today. If you do not already follow God, it begins soon after you surrender to a relationship with Jesus. Your legacy of spiritual impact is worked at every day, as you help others to love Jesus, follow Him and godly principles, and serve other believers and non-believers. Specifically, it describes the spiritual legacy. This means that if you do not have offspring, or if your children do not have children, a spiritual legacy is still available to you. God does not grant any human the ability to know when life on earth will end, so every day has the possibility of being the last.

Most people wonder who will remember them after life ends. The answer depends on a number of factors: the magnitude of their impact, what history records, whether they lived their destinies, and if they did it in a way that inspires others. promises everyone an opportunity to be remembered, but the type of remembrance is not the same for all people. The verse says, "Many of those who sleep in the dust of the earth shall awake, some to everlasting life and some to shame and everlasting contempt. Those who are wise will shine like the brightness of the heavens, and those who lead many to righteousness, like the stars, will shine forever and ever." Those who have the hope of shining like stars in the afterlife are believers who "lead many to the right paths"; in other words, who lead others to Jesus Christ as their Lord and Savior and mentor them in the Christian faith.

CHAPTER 32

Conclusion

I also hope they will serve you as a resource for family discussions. To the best of my ability, I have tried to make this information available to be understood on various levels. I have drawn from scriptures, as well as from history, current events, and even popular culture with the intent to demonstrate that divine purpose is a relevant and pertinent concept for each and every one of us. Ultimately, this teleseminar and the following collection of messages in this volume are about you. I am confident that each of you will be touched in some personal way and be reminded that the divinity within you yearns to discover your calling in God's plan. May God bless you in this effort.

I believe that many of your questions will be answered during the teleseminar and watching the DVD, but if they are not, I would be delighted to hear from you. In fact, I consider you to be a part of this work. Please let me know of your thoughts, insights, inspirations, and, yes, even your disagreements. I suggest that you and others go to the website to submit these important communications. You will find most of the relevant information there about these messages, as well as beautiful music.

First, let me suggest that you listen to these messages in their entirety. Many of the messages in the series were recorded in a fifty-minute format to meet the needs of both the Good4U Marketing Corporation and those of you who may have listened to the teleseminar live. The thirty-minute or fifty-minute time designation is simply for convenience in placing the conversation on radio broadcasts. I have purposefully designed the material for this volume to be presented in forty-five-minute talks to allow time for a question and answer session at the end. The questions asked by those who listened to each of the messages will probably be ones you and people like you would like information about as well. Your listening time is valuable and training your ear to catch everything said plus the added information in the question and answer segment will be an important investment in your spiritual education.

Thank you for listening to my messages in the teleseminar series, Divine Purpose: Discovering Your Calling in God's Plan. I recognize that you have numerous calls on your time and pray you will find it worthwhile to have listened to what I have been inspired to present, for your life now and in the future. I hope the messages will encourage and uplift you.